Five Dresses:

Girl's Guide to Effortless Chic

BY: SUSANBSTERN

This book is dedicated to my daughter and to all the young ladies with whom I've had the pleasure to know and teach.

~MODERN ETIQUETTE~

~ADVICE I'D GIVE MY YOUNGER SELF~

~ENTERTAINING~

~STYLE STRATEGIES~

~HOW TO BUILD A WARDROBE~

The following information and advice is part of Volume 2 in the series Five Dresses.
Volume 1 is available as either eBook or paperback on Amazon.com.   Volume 3 is coming soon – Seamingly French

~MODERN ETIQUETTE~

"Etiquette, a fancy word for common kindness"
    ~ Elsa Maxwell

The Art of the Thank You Note

I hope this art is not lost, but I am becoming increasingly worried it might.   My general rule of thumb is to write a thank you note when receiving a gift of any kind. Even after just typing that, I remember the thank you note I got a few weeks ago. It was by far, the worst thank you note I have ever received. Written by an adult, I could have sworn it was attributed to a child.   It stated:
Dear Susan, (my card to her was from my entire family)
Thank you for the gift. We will use it often.
Signed, Terrible Thank you note writer

I could not believe my eyes. To top it all off, the note was addressed to me on the envelope by a printed sticker. Apparently, writing my name on the card was too taxing.   A printed sticker would be acceptable if the note had been mailed. But this note was simply handed to me.

For an adult, writing the note becomes an art. One opens the letter with proper salutation and immediately thanks for the gift. Then, you write a line or two about how sweet and thoughtful it was of them to give you the gift. If possible, describe how you will use the gift and for what purpose. Lastly, mention something personal about your relationship with them. One might add, it was so wonderful chatting with you the other night or it was just lovely to see how great you look and spend time with you again. Close the note with a simple « Thanks again for thinking of me » and sign your name. Your note is easy, personal and to the point. I am committed; this art will not be lost.

~When overwhelmed with Thank you notes to write (for a graduation, shower, wedding, etc.), take your time and write a few every day. If you attempt to personalize and write more than 3 or 4 a day, they will all sound the same and the sentiment will be gone. Begin the day after the event with one or two notes and then progress each day. Simply go down your list or prioritize with those closest to you.

~Email, Hashtag, & Social Media etiquette~

Just a few years ago, this entire sector of etiquette was being established. It feels as though something new is introduced each day with technology. Questions remain as to the proper behavior when new technology emerges. One thing stays a constant, though, when in doubt, be formal.

The art of the Email

There is a very big difference in sending an email to a professor/employer and to a friend or family member. Some people use the same informal address with both and this is terribly incorrect. Don't forget that even though email is instant, one must still treat it like a letter when writing a teacher, professor, or future employer. Use a simple opening, ask how they are, state your purpose or question and finally, close. When emailing a friend or family member, no opening or closing is really necessary and is at your discretion.

The art of the Hashtag

I debated on the title for this section. Is the hashtag really becoming an art? And the answer is yes. To poetically craft the perfect hashtag is better left to someone in marketing or fashion journalism.

The point of this topic is to emphasize when the hashtag is beneficial and when it is detrimental. The hashtag is beneficial when promoting a product, brand or trying to categorize several items together in a search. The hashtag is inappropriate for use at a wedding when the bride and groom might want to keep their photos private. The same decorum applies to a new parent when you take a picture of their child. Certain occasions require discretion and guidance from the ones who are the center of attention. Always follow their lead. If no lead has been given, email or mail pictures after the event.

Social Media Etiquette

Posting to social media has become so automatic that we often forget to ask permission when posting certain photos. If you're dear friends and know they wouldn't mind a smiling picture post from your lunch, post away.

However, please exercise caution when posting pictures of other people's children or pictures from an evening out. Some people prefer to keep their children off of other people's social media and this request should be respected.

Don't post a picture from an event that might embarrass a friend or colleague. These posts are seen by many and discovered by the masses, including your employer or coach, etc. Some things are better kept un-photographed or hidden away in a real, hardback photo album.

~ Social Dilemmas solved~

What to do when the food at an event is terrible: whether at Christmas dinner or a friend's cocktail party

Unless you are allergic or the food is literally inedible, one must eat a small acceptable amount. If you host/hostess questions you, just advise them that you ate a bit too much of a favorite indulgence mid-afternoon and don't seem to be hungry at present. If your host or hostess wants you to take home food, please take it. That is always the polite thing to do. Even if you know you'll put it in the trash later, take it. Write a note when you get home and send the next day with a word of thanks.

You accidentally posted a picture, tweet, or status online and regret it.

Delete immediately. Hope and pray no one saw it, but assume that some might have. When in doubt if that you posted was okay, just delete. If someone posted a picture or said something about you that is not flattering, kindly ask them to delete or remove.

You lied to get out of going to social event and your plan backfired, you got busted.

This will happen, no matter how good you think your little white lie was. I am always too paranoid to lie about illness, since I'm sure I will get caught looming in Nordstrom among the shoes or that karma will catch me and I'll really get ill. There will be times when you receive an invitation and it's for something lovely and you want to attend, but are just worn out. That is an okay time to lie, in my opinion. If it's a close friend, just tell them the truth. Not to do this often, but life can get too complicated and exhausting and if you need a rest, take one. Just make sure if you get caught, you are ready to explain yourself.

How to get out of a never-ending conversation

It's always lovely to chat and catch up. I once had a co-worker who would orbit me like a planet and talk about superfluous information for what seemed like days. I tried many different techniques to leave those conversations and the only thing that seemed to work was slowly backing up and pretending to be in a hurry. I don't recommend this technique unless you're in a dire situation, but it will work. The best way to exit a conversation that is endless is to try and find a moment of space and politely say something along the lines of "I really need to use the ladies room" or " I'm so sorry, I must go or I'll be late to an appointment. It was lovely chatting with you!"

How to handle an unwanted gift.
This is easy. Accept the gift. Say thank you. Gush over the gift and then, send a thank you note. Do what you wish with the gift after you get home. And never tell the gift bearer what you did. If it's someone that lives close by, keep the gift in storage and when you know they are dropping by, set it out. This is inevitable. And if the gifter comes to your house unannounced and asks where the item is, a polite excuse might be, "It's still in storage from our move." Or "I placed it in the study/bedroom and am still trying to find the perfect spot for it." This last argument is not quite as convincing, but still worth a try.

If you hurt a friend, lied, or otherwise, just apologize.
For some people, it is the toughest thing to do. It will be awkward and it will be difficult, but the good thing is, it will be over soon. It will be in the past and things will get better. If you are at fault, admit it, apologize and move on. Looming guilt is much worse and will literally give you wrinkles from worry. No one wants wrinkles if we can avoid them. Besides, you will feel much better when it's over.

You have an event or party and there are certain people in your group of friends with whom you don't particularly get along.
Do you invite them all? Or invite only your nearest and dearest? This is a tricky situation and will really depend on the type of event. If it's a general party, for a graduation or cocktail party, and will be a big event, why not invite all? If it's a small party, for a birthday or a wedding, it's your choice for the guest list. Keep in mind, word spreads and feelings might be hurt.

~ADVICE I WOULD GIVE MY YOUNGER SELF~

"Playing dress up begins at age five and truly never ends"
    ~Kate Spade

~HOW TO BE YOUR OWN ADVOCATE~

There are times to be silent and times to raise your voice. How do I choose the right moment? As time goes by and you get more experience, your instinct will tell you the correct answer. Don't be afraid of your voice or what others will think and always trust your instinct.

Be silent when:
~Someone says something out of ignorance, but you know they mean well. (For example, when I was pregnant, I heard so many comments of "you're getting so big!" I know people meant well, but how in the world does one reply to that?)
~You know you're wrong. Don't fight it.
~Someone's grammar is incorrect, even if it bothers you.
~You can't change their mind, no matter how hard you try.
~Don't be so quick to judge others and shame others. We all have a story.

Raise your voice when:
~You are being bothered and feel uncomfortable.
~Someone has said something mean to you. Someone has been disrespectful to you.
~You get a funny feeling in your gut; trust your instinct.
~You don't understand and need to ask questions. (This is especially critical when signing contracts. Don't be pushed into signing something. Always read the fine print.
~You feel someone needs help.

~HEALTH & BEAUTY HABITS~

~Drink lots of water, especially first thing in the morning. Some say it's best to drink hot water with lemon and a dash of honey. I am always hopeful I will have time for that and I never do. I always start my day with a big glass of water. Before all else, drink water. Add taste drops (like Crystal Light) to it if you prefer. Your body will thank you.

~Wash your face every night. No matter how exhausted you are or how tired you are, always wash your face. Use face lotion appropriate for your skin tone/type and age and also apply to your neck. The hands and neck can reveal one's age. There are so many creams, serums and lotions on the market. Just find the one you like and stick to a regime. Your 35-year-old self will thank your younger self. I promise.

~Have a positive attitude. A smile goes a long way and can brighten someone's day. Start by brightening your own day first!

~Take a break from your contacts. Invest in a darling pair of glasses. Wear them from time to time and give your eyes a rest.

~As much as I preach about activity and keeping your body active, rest is just as important. Take naps.   Take a day off or a few hours off and do nothing.

~If you only have two minutes for your make-up, apply concealer, blush, lip gloss and mascara. Mascara will always save you from looking dreary.

~Take care of your hands and feet. Often, women forget to touch-up pedicures or manicures and ironically, that's one of the first things someone notices.

~Lotion, lotion, lotion. My grandmother had lotion in every room in her house and now I know why.   The more you lather up on the lotion, the better your skin will look and feel. On that note, apply sunscreen. Always.

~Take your vitamins. Talk to your doctor about which ones are best for you and take them religiously. Some people might need more vitamin D or Calcium. Follow doctor's orders.

~Every month or so, take a look at all of your beauty products and cosmetics and throw them out accordingly. Cosmetics all have different shelf lives and one should pay close attention to the dates. It's always good to abide by those dates since you use cosmetics on your skin and eyes everyday. Allure magazine has a great slideshow on their website about when beauty products expire and how long their shelf life lasts.

~OTHER ETIQUETTE CONUNDRUMS~

~If a friend or date doesn't call or text and they are running more than 15 minutes behind, there is a problem. In this day and age of voice texting, if they can't spare 30 seconds to send you a note, they don't respect you or your time. Which brings me to, always call if you're going to be more than 5 minutes late. It's really a respectful courtesy to the person you're meeting.

~ Remember that your parents were once young. You might not understand them all of the time and that's okay. But they were once where you are. They didn't have all of the technology, but they had the same feelings.

~Life is short. Don't waste your time or energy on people who don't give you a second thought or aren't considerate of you. Respect is a two way street and relationships should be built on mutual respect.
Lavish your time on projects and people you love.

~Be kind to others. Even those you don't care for. You never know when you might need their help or you see them again. You will never regret being nice to someone.

~Take care of yourself. I have a general 3-day rule for myself physically. If I have a headache for a day, I don't worry. If it goes on for three days, I call the doctor. The same goes for anything else related to my health. One day is a coincidence, two days is ironic and three days is a problem.

~Sometimes the 3-day rule applies to other areas of your life as well. If I am worrying constantly about something and can't get it out of my mind for 3 straight days, I confront the issue or person in a polite way.
*This applies to shopping as well. Our lives are so busy that if you're still thinking of an item three days later; just go buy it.

~Sometimes you just need to talk to someone and sometimes you just need to be alone. Make sure you are articulate and nice in your request if you're asking someone to leave and have your alone time.

~ It's okay to turn off your phone and pretend it's the early 90's again! Look at a clock for the time, read a magazine during the TV commercials or just go for a walk. You'd be surprised how therapeutic it can be to have your technology on pause for a bit. Experts do say it is wise to turn off all devices a half hour before bed for better sleep.

~We are blessed to have first world problems a lot of the time. But they can be overwhelming and quite stressful. When I'm stressed or going through a rough time, I remind myself I am lucky to have first world problems. This works most of the time and for the other times when it doesn't work, I just remind myself it will be over soon.

~When dealing with in-laws, blood talks to blood. My mother told me this the day I got married and I have followed her advice. For those important or tricky conversations, don't get in the middle unless it is imperative (for example, if kids are involved).

~Build a gift closet and a card closet. Next time you go to Target, browse through the cheap card section, the dollar bins and get an array of cards and keep them for those last minute occasions or things you forget. The gift closet is equally essential. There will be moments when you forgot to buy a gift for a last minute party. There will be moments when you think you have wrapping paper and then realize you're out and have to run to the store. Gift closets are genius. Always keep a stock of cards, gift-wrap, gift bags and gift items on hand. After all, isn't that what a sale is for? It's okay to buy that gift in February for next Christmas. Just put it in the closet.

~ MONEY MANAGEMENT~

No one likes to deal with the important, serious stuff in life. It's not enjoyable looking at your budget, but it is a necessity. If you take care of your financial life, you will feel more confident about other areas. Below is a short guide to a few things every gal needs to know about when it comes to money.

Student Loans: When you graduate college, you might have a student loan. If you don't have a student loan, congratulations; please don't rub it in other's faces. Try to get the lowest possible interest on your student loan and explore payment options. Some plans will give you the option of a graduated payment plan. This might be best if you graduate college and are not earning much. A graduated payment plan means that you will pay a small amount for a few years and then the amount will increase every few years until it is paid in full. This is good for those students starting out in a new career and trying to create their budget. Explore other options if they are available. Student loan debt is not bad debt. Just remember to pay it on time and pay every month.

Credit Cards: Use them wisely. Realize that it is entirely too easy to use a credit card and live in denial about paying it back. Save the credit cards for big purchases that you need to make soon and know you will pay off quickly. I always carry a credit card and will even use it for small purchases if I don't feel comfortable using my debit card. Keep track of these purchases and pay them as soon as you can. If you have credit card debt, make a plan to pay it off as soon as you are able.

Savings Account: Experts say it is best to have three months of life style expenses saved in your savings account for emergencies. I bet these experts didn't have a shoe addiction. Regardless, put aside a good amount of money in your savings for each paycheck and stick to it. If it's 10 percent; super. If it's only $100 a month; great. Just make a plan to build up your savings and don't touch it unless an emergency comes along. And by emergency, I mean you lose your job or the washing machine breaks and you need a new one. Unfortunately, a shoe sale at Neiman Marcus is not classified as a real emergency. This breaks my heart to type, but it's true.

Retirement Account: When you begin working, you will be offered the chance to contribute to your retirement account. No matter how small the sum you contribute, just contribute. I didn't do this for many years and I had regrets. My husband told me (before we got engaged) that he wouldn't marry me until I set up a retirement fund. The next day, I went to Human Resources. It's good to invest aggressively when you're young. Remember to read over the material and ask questions. Ask friends who might know a lot about it and do your research before turning in the paperwork.

~WORDS OF ENCOURAGEMENT~
Being Your Own Cheerleader
There are times in life when you must be your own cheerleader. This is not to say you don't have support. This is just a word of advice for the moments when you want to give up, are tired, stressed, or frustrated. You can have all the friends in the world support you, but in the end, it's your attitude that will help you feel better.

~Mental Health days are important. Sometimes your world (not THE world) needs to stop and you need a break. Just to look at pretty things and window shop, go to a yoga class, or take a walk. Make sure you take these at the appropriate time, though. Don't just take a mental health day because you don't want to work or didn't meet a deadline. Sometimes our mental health days can come from canceling all of your plans on a Saturday and watching a marathon of House of Cards or Gossip Girl. Sometimes you just need to cut yourself some slack and recharge your batteries.

~You will succeed. Yes, you, the discouraged one who just cried her eyes out because she is working so diligently and doesn't seem to make progress. You will succeed. Believe it will happen and make it happen.

~When in doubt, just be nice. Smile. And continue on with your business. See above reference about when to speak and when to be silent. There will be times when people say or do inappropriate things and instead of wasting your time on explanations, just smile and move on.

~ENTERTAINING~

"Spring is Nature's Way of Saying, 'Let's Party!'"
~Robin Williams

Parties and get-togethers can be fun, just make sure you plan accordingly so you can enjoy the party as well and not have any stress. Little details listed below should lend in making your party spectacular and one you can enjoy. Guests remember little details. The most important thing about any party is making your guests feel welcome and special. If you do that, your parties will always get the good RSVPs*

~WHAT TO HAVE ON HAND WHEN ENTERTAINING~

For my very first cocktail party as a single gal, I thought I was completely prepared. Thank goodness for my husband (then newly dating) who brought me some essentials I had not thought about. I had enough wine and food, of course, but I didn't think about having the following:
Ice
Extra water glasses
Bottled Water
Sodas and tea (in case your guests don't prefer alcohol)

~Before having guests over, make sure at a minimum, these two areas are spotless. The kitchen counters and the bathroom. People linger in the kitchen and the bathroom is the only place where they are alone. This is why multipurpose wipes were invented. Take a few wipes and clean those surfaces. In ten minutes, things look spotless. If you have more time, do a better clean. But for a last minute event, this tip works well.

~Clean off an area for people to place coats and handbags. That's the first thing people will look for after they greet you. A bench near the doorway is a great idea or simply take their items and place in a nearby room. Always tell your guests where you are placing their things, as they might need them later.

~Make sure you speak to each guest you've invited for at least a few minutes. This is easy with a small crowd. You want your guests to feel special. Guests won't mind if food runs out, but they will remember a gracious host that was glad to have them attend.

*R.S.V.P. is French for Répondez, s'il vous plaît. This translates to "respond, please." So many people are unaware of this and write an additional "please" on an invitation.

~10 MINUTE THROW TOGETHER MEALS~

When I was single, my oven was used for storage. And then I met a boy who could cook. My mother then said to me, "You come from a long line of amazing cooks including a French chef. Surely, you can make a meal for him, too."

And so, I began my foodie fascination. Below are some meals and appetizers you can literally throw together.

~Bruschetta (needs: loaf of bread, fresh basil, fresh tomatoes, mozzarella, and balsamic vinegar)

Slice loaf into one inch thick slices. Place tomato slices and mozzarella slices on each piece and drizzle with balsamic. Flavored balsamic vinegars work very well with this too.

~Meat/cheese/fruit plate (also known as a charcuterie plate)...(needs: salami or summer sausage, grapes, a hard cheese - like parmesan and a soft cheese – like camembert)

Have the butcher slice or buy the salami and sausage pre-sliced. Take caution with the cheeses and make sure you have the correct cheese knife. Some places will take care of slicing the cheese for you.

~Quesadilla: use rotisserie or leftover grilled chicken

Sprinkle tortillas with cooked chicken and cheese, adding beans if you wish. Place in a hot skillet with oil. Leave it alone until the tortilla is cooked and then flip to the other side. Use a plate to help you flip the tortilla. Place a plate on top of the skillet, put your right hand on the plate and with your left hand flip the skillet. The quesadilla will be on your plate and you can gently slide the quesadilla back on the skillet to heat the other side. When it is done, you can cut into various pieces, squeeze a dash of lime over it and sprinkle with cilantro. Sour cream and cherry tomatoes are an added bonus.

~Fresh veggie for crudité

Carrots, broccoli, and cauliflower are all common for this type of plate and most people will serve a sour cream and onion or ranch dip with the vegetables. These veggies are safe as they do well cold or even if they've been out for a few hours. Why not spice it up a bit and use a flavored hummus with sugar snap peas, red or yellow peppers and radishes. Adding some olives and cheese makes a plate even more perfection.

~For the quickest throw together, just grab a loaf of bread, salami plate, various jams and jellies, soft cheeses

What to always have on hand to make a meal in a hurry?

It never fails. A friend or family member has called and wants to come over around lunch or dinnertime. Take out is always nice, but impressing them with your "faux" culinary skills is even better. These meals might take a little more time, but they are worth it and healthy.

~Chicken pesto pasta salad~15 minutes prep maximum
Pesto
Sun dried tomatoes (or cherry tomatoes)
Pasta
Chicken (pre-cooked from the grocery store)

Cook pasta to al dente, throw in pre-cooked chicken (or grilled chicken) and tomatoes with pesto. Add arugula if you'd like or peppers. A healthy and easy meal in minutes makes you look like a pro.

Quick rosemary chicken & veggies ~35 minutes to cook
Marinate chicken for a minimum of 15 minutes to 3 hours in lemon and chopped fresh rosemary. Grill on each side for 6-7 minutes. One could also make this in the oven. Just place in the pan with some sliced red onions, small potatoes and cherry tomatoes. Roast at 375 degrees for 35-40 minutes and flip veggies halfway through the process. A perfect, easy and quick meal!

Cilantro lime rice →
Cook rice according to instructions (although I suggest a quick soak and then drain of the water before cooking). When the rice is done, add some chopped cilantro, and squeeze of a lime. This goes perfectly with grilled meat or simple kabobs. Add avocado, fresh pineapple and some fresh tomato for some color.

Almond covered chicken →
Instead of breaded chicken, put some almonds (I prefer roasted tamari) in a food processor and blend until fine. Place two bowls near a hot skillet with oil in it. Take your thinly sliced chicken and place it in the first bowl (one egg mixed with a dash of milk) and coat, then place in the second bowl (almond grounds). One the chicken is coated on both sides, place in the hot pan. Be sure not to overcrowd the pan. Once cooked on both sides, place a small salad of tomato, cucumber, basil and balsamic on the side.

~STYLE STRATEGIES~
If the shoe fits, buy it.
Or as Rachel Zoe says, "Here's my rule about shoes: Buy them."

The biggest Dos and Don'ts and when to break all the rules.

••

Please don't wear.....

~...Crop tops: let's face it. Unless you have a full time trainer, crop tops should be avoided past your late 20's. If you've got it and can flaunt it, go ahead. Honestly, though, the most flattering look for a woman is a blouse or tee shirt that is long enough to stop at mid-hip. This is universally flattering.

~...Anything that shows your bra strap. There is a reason a strapless bra was invented. I urge you to go to a store where you feel comfortable and get a proper bra fitting. One should do this every few years or as your body and/or weight changes. Buy several in different colors.

~....Work-out clothes to leave the house. Unless you are actually jogging to the store (I admit, I have done this from time to time and had my husband pick me up when I finished shopping), please refrain and keep the workout clothes on the street running or in the gym.

~...Leggings are meant to be worn with tunics or long, tailored shirts. Cover your bum. Leave something to the imagination. The person behind you at the grocery store or shopping malldoes not need to see the curve of your bottom and the type of under garments you're wearing since your leggings are too tight.

~...Matchy Matchy clothes. There's only so much beige one can handle in a suit. I'm talking about the suits that come pre-coordinated for you and are made of cheap fabric. This is no longer the 80's. And on that note, please, no shoulder pads. It's fun to watch a throwback movie like 9 to 5, but let's the leave it in the classics.

••

And when to break the rules.....

"If you put something together and it doesn't look good, the fashion police isn't going to come take you away. And even if they do, you might have some fun in jail."

~Iris Apfel

~Mixing prints and textures can work within reason. I've seen women take striped tops and patterned floral scarves to a new level of fabulous dressing all because the textures and colors were similar and it was absolutely stunning.

~Wear white anytime of year you wish. Who cares what season it is? Wear white in a beautiful coat or shift dress. Just make sure your fabrics are weather appropriate. Keep white linen in spring and summer, for obvious reasons of warmth.

~Who says you should only wear one necklace? Pile it on for a big event. Layer some pearls and topknot your hair.

~Denim with denim. A truly stylish girl can pair an entire outfit in denim and make it work. Accessories can complete the outfit and make the denim look chic.

~Sparkle and sequins are just for evening. Wear sequins for brunch.

~Mixing gold and silver jewelry. Why commit to one style? Mix it all with rose gold if you wish.

Clothing storage

~ Fold sweaters and dry clean, if necessary

~Invest in nice, wooden hangers for your blouses, shirts and slacks. Ikea and Target sell them in groups of 4-5 for very little money. Start stocking up each time you make a visit or buy a ton of hangers at once.

~Either keep shoes in boxes (with pictures for easy reference) or standing upright on a shelf or closet floor. Never, ever leave them in a pile.

~Boots must be kept upright. You can buy the inserts so your gorgeous suede boots stay upright or simply roll up some newspaper or magazine and place them in the boot.

~Every few months; clean out the closet. It's always a good idea to either donate or sell what you haven't worn in a year. My general rule is, if I haven't worn it in 6 months and don't plan to wear it, it goes to someone else.

~Make sure you clearly label boxes with hats.

~Fold scarves; especially the silk ones.

~Keep a clothing refresher (such as Febreeze) on hand in the closet as well. Anytime I wear a scarf, I spray it with a clothing refresher before storing again. Some items can be worn several times before sending to the cleaners.

~HOW TO BUILD A WARDROBE~

"Buy less, choose well."
>~Vivienne Westwood

~Making the inexpensive look chic~

  We've all been there. Staring at a closet full of clothes and thinking, "I need more clothes, none of these work." What we are really saying is, "I can't find clothes for who I am today and what I feel." Some days, you feel like a dress and wearing pink, others you feel like black from head to toe with a dash of red. I have had moments where I wanted to throw my entire closet out and start from scratch. While that is extreme, I do feel it important to go through your clothing inventory every few months and if you haven't worn it in a year (or the past season), it's time to sell online or donate. Besides, you could use the tax credit, right? After you've done the purge, as I call it, it's time to build a wish list! Take a look at your closet and decide what basics below you need or want and slowly re-build your closet. This will take time, more than likely, and you probably want to look at your budget first. Below are pieces listed by investment and buy me now pieces. Investment pieces are worth the money and quality. These are the kind of pieces you will hand down to someone one day. The buy me now pieces are the ones you can get at anytime and probably find at a good deal. I also call these pieces so cheap, it's like they are giving them away.

I'm not providing prices on the investment versus buy me now pieces. Your budget will dictate that. Decide what you're able to spend and work within that frame. It will come together soon enough.

~Investment pieces~

~A good winter coat

...choose a bold or neutral solid color. A good quality coat will last you for years. I would stay away from suede as a primary coat material unless it's one of many coats you are buying. Choose a good durable fabric that will stand up against cold and snow.

~A great fitting pair of jeans,

the kind that you can wear and always feel fabulous

~The perfect sheath dress...

.the one that fits you like a glove. I'd go with a beige or navy, but pick your favorite color and anytime you have a party or event and think you have nothing to wear, this will save you.

~Nude heels

these are the heels that work with any ensemble. They are not too high and not too low, I'd stick with 3 inch. Ones that you can wear all day with any outfit and they are not painful.

~A gorgeous silk scarf with bright colors and a bold pattern. Scour the vintage stores for Hermes and snatch one up if you get lucky. Otherwise, find a nice, silk bold color scarf that will pair with any suit or tee shirt and jeans you have.

~Buy Me Now Pieces~

~A black turtleneck, this will go with almost anything and can be dressed up with jewelry or a scarf.

~The perfect white t-shirt, wear with jeans and heels or shorts and flip flops. Proper accessories make the statement with a simple tee shirt.

~Statement necklace, the chunky, bold color type of necklace.

~White button down blouse, the tailored ones from Gap and J Crew are nice. Brooks brothers carries some fabulous ones too.

~A gorgeous cocktail ring, the kind that makes you feel fabulous just by slipping it on. Even though you got it for $25 at Nordstrom Rack. Sometimes you just need something fancy.

-Tank tops, no matter your age or size, tank tops are always good to have on hand when layering. If you don't want to bear arms, then simply put a blazer over the tank top with a beautiful necklace or scarf. One can always layer a simple tank under a blouse or wear alone in the summertime.

The Key Five pieces you need for every wardrobe:
Building will take time, but once you get there, it will be worth it.
Shoes → flats, boots, heels, flip flops, sandals
Handbags → weekend bag, tote bag, satchel, clutch, shoulder bag
Dresses → sheath, shift, maxi, cocktail dress, simple cotton slip on dress
Jewelry → cocktail ring, statement necklace, bracelet, everyday earrings, eveningwear earrings

~BUILDING THE GENTLEMAN'S WARDROBE~

The gentleman's wardrobe can be as simple or as complicated as one might want. Beginning with the formal part of a man's life, every man needs at least three suits. These three suits will carry him from job interviews, major meetings, church, funerals and springtime/summer.

Essentials for the men's suiting wardrobe
3 suits: one black, one beige, one navy (stripes optional)
3 shoes: black (either lace up or slip on), dark brown and light colored or beige
3 ties or bow ties: shade of red/orange, green/blue and grey/black

Socks are a great place for a man to express personality. Vibrant sock colors and patterns are a fun way to jazz up a suit for work.

Every man needs a good loafer or deck shoe, which he can pair with polo shirts, flat front pleat shorts.

Volume 3 of the Five Dresses series is coming soon.

Five Dresses: Seamingly French (available June 2015)

www.ingramcontent.com/pod-product-compliance
Lightning Source LLC
Chambersburg PA
CBHW070944290526
45795CB00003B/1139